For Bert and Chloé

Fun-to-Read Picture Books have been grouped into three approximate readability levels by Bernice and Cliff Moon. Yellow books are suitable for beginners; red books for readers acquiring first fluency; blue books for more advanced readers.

This book has been assessed as Stage 9 according to *Individualised Reading*, by Bernice and Cliff Moon, published by The Centre for the Teaching of Reading, University of Reading School of Education.

First published 1986 by
Walker Books Ltd
184-192 Drummond Street
London NW1 3HP

Text © 1986 Barry Tomblin
Illustrations © 1986 Gill Tomblin

First printed 1986
Printed and bound by
L.E.G.O., Vicenza, Italy

British Library Cataloguing in Publication Data
Tomblin, Barry
Jenny's buried treasure.—(Fun-to-read
picture books)
1. Readers—1950-
I. Title   II. Tomblin, Gill   III. Series
428.6   PE1119

ISBN 0-7445-0537-2

Jenny's
Buried Treasure

WRITTEN BY
Barry Tomblin

ILLUSTRATED BY
Gill Tomblin

WALKER BOOKS
LONDON

'Why are you digging that hole?'
Peter asked his sister.
'I'm burying treasure,' replied Jenny.
'What kind of treasure?' asked Peter.
'Secret treasure,' said Jenny.

When she had finished digging,
Jenny put a brown paper parcel into the hole.
She filled the hole with soil and
patted the soil down flat.
'There!' said Jenny. 'My treasure
will be safe now.'

'But how will you find it again?' asked Peter.
'Easy,' said Jenny. 'I'll make a map.'
So Jenny drew an X on a piece of paper
to show where the treasure lay.
Then she marked in every footstep as
she paced her way up the garden to the house.
'There!' said Jenny when the map was finished.
'My treasure will be safe now.'

'If somebody found that map,' said Peter,
'they could dig up your treasure and take it.'
'Not if I hide it,' said Jenny, and
she put the map in a drawer in the sideboard
and locked the drawer.
'There!' said Jenny. 'My treasure
will be safe now.'

'But if somebody found the key,' said Peter,
'they could open the drawer and
find the map. Then they could dig up
your treasure and take it.'
'Not if I hide the key,' said Jenny, and
she dropped the key into a little plastic box
that sat on the mantlepiece and closed the lid.
'There!' said Jenny. 'My treasure
will be safe now.'

'But if somebody opened the box,' said Peter,
'they would find the key. And if somebody
found the key, they could open the drawer. And
if somebody opened the drawer, they would find
the map. And if somebody found the map,
they could dig up your treasure and take it!'

'Not if I guard the box,' said Jenny, 'and don't let anyone near it.'

So Jenny wrapped up the box.
She put the box on a shelf in her room.
Then she sat and watched it for a long,
long time.
Just when she thought she couldn't watch
it any longer, she heard her mother calling.
'Jenny!' shouted Jenny's mum. 'Grandad's
here for tea.'

Jenny and Peter ran to greet him.
'Happy birthday, Grandad!' they both cried.
'Yes, happy birthday,' said Mum and Dad.

After tea Grandad opened his presents.

From Jenny's dad he got a scarf.

Jenny's mum gave him a pair of gloves.

Peter gave him a hat with a pom-pom on top.

Even Samson the dog gave him a great big lick.

But when Grandad opened Jenny's parcel,

all he found was a little plastic box.

'Is this my birthday present?' asked Grandad.

'No,' said Jenny. 'Look inside.'

Grandad opened the little plastic box and
held up a key.
'Is this key my present?' asked Grandad.
'No,' said Jenny. 'It opens the sideboard drawer.'
Grandad opened the sideboard drawer and
found a map.
'Is this map my present?' asked Grandad.
'No,' said Jenny. 'See where it leads you.'

So Grandad counted out the footsteps that
led back down the garden to the spot marked X
and almost fell head over heels into
an empty hole in the ground.
'My treasure!' screamed Jenny. 'Somebody's
taken my treasure!'

Just then Samson came padding out from
behind the hedge. He was wagging his tail and
carrying a parcel in his mouth.
'My treasure!' shouted Jenny. 'Samson
took my treasure.'
'Good boy,' chuckled Grandad, patting
Samson on the head. 'You saved me a dig.'

Grandad untied the brown paper parcel.
Inside he found a ship in a bottle.
'Is this ship my present?' he asked.
'Yes,' said Jenny proudly. 'It's a
 pirate ship that hunts for pirate gold.'
'What a wonderful present,' said Grandad.
'I shall treasure it always.'